Say What?

Say What?

Here's How You Can Say and Write it Better

Janet Carmichael

iUniverse, Inc.
New York   Bloomington

iUniverse books may be ordered through booksellers or by contacting:

iUniverse
1663 Liberty Drive
Bloomington, IN 47403
www.iuniverse.com
1-800-Authors (1-800-288-4677)

Because of the dynamic nature of the Internet, any Web addresses or links contained in this book may have changed since publication and may no longer be valid. The views expressed in this work are solely those of the author and do not necessarily reflect the views of the publisher, and the publisher hereby disclaims any responsibility for them.

ISBN: 978-1-4502-0635-8 (sc)
ISBN: 978-1-4502-0636-5 (ebook)

Library of Congress Control Number: 2010901239

Printed in the United States of America

iUniverse rev. date: 03/16/2010

Table of Contents

Introduction vii

1. The Teeth, the Lips, the Tip of the Tongue:

- The Importance of Good Articulation 1
- Some that Suffer in Silence 3
- Exercises 7

2. Let's Wage a War on "Words"

- Non-Words 12
- Malapropisms 16
- Colloquialisms. 17
- Review and Practice Time 18

3. Render Results with Rules:

- Grammar: A definition 19
- Grammar: Two Branches of Study 20
- The Sentence: A complete thought expressed in words. 20
- Subject and Predicate 21
- The Verb is the action word 22
- Review and Practice Time 23

4. Rules Still Rule the Roost

- The Object of the Verb 26
- The Extension of the Verb 31
- Analysis of the Simple Sentence 32
- The Verb Revisited 32
- Review and Practice Time 34

5. Words Need a Relationship

- The Parts of Speech   38
- Why Words Change   43
- How Tense Changes Words   43
- How Number Changes Words   45
- Review and Practice Time   52

6. A Choice of Words:

- Choose with Care   56
- Why Lay and Lie Cause Trouble   59
- Review and Practice Time   64

7. Pull the Plug on Poor Punctuation

- The Apostrophe (')   67
- The Apostrophe in Contractions   68
- The Apostrophe to Show Possession   69
- The Apostrophe that Pronouns Never Need   70
- The Ellipsis Dots   72
- Review and Practice Time   74

8. Epilogue

- That Time of Day   75
- New Horizons   76

Answers to Review and Practice Time   79

Introduction

One of the songs the English actor, Rex Harrison, sang when he played Professor Higgins in *My Fair Lady* began like this: "Why won't the English teach their children how to speak?" I think he sang in exasperation as young Eliza Doolittle's voice rang out in her own inimitable style as she communicated with other vendors outside the opera house. Today I ask the question with a difference. I ask, "Why won't parents and our institutions of learning teach our children how to speak?"

It is not my intention to lay the blame solely at the feet of parents. Others bear an equal responsibility. Everyone knows that most parents try to teach their children how to speak, how to write, as a matter of fact, how to do a number of things well. Alas! Children do not always follow parental advice; but prefer to be part of the "culture" they find within their different peer groups. No child wants to be different from the others in the group. The mores must, at all cost, be adhered to.

The fact remains, too, that we have among us many children and young adults who speak exactly as their parents do. That could be a bad thing and it could be a good thing. It all depends.

It is, therefore, with some boldness—and mild trepidation—that I attempt to deal with some of the errors in speech and writing with which I have been regaled during my several years as an educator, trainer, and concerned member of society. I do this primarily for selfish reasons; the main one being to lessen my intense discomfort every time I hear or see the language "slaughtered". But I am also doing this for the love of the people in our society—young and not-so-young—who genuinely want to improve their oral and written communication skills regardless of the pressure they might endure from their peers and others to be like everyone else. In everyone, I see such promise, a hope for better things to come, a glimpse of what I call that elusive lexical utopia.

Many of the wonderful, young minds in our midst do not yet realize how important it is to cultivate these skills. They are unaware of the extent to which such skills can and will contribute to their marketability in an increasingly difficult job market. They are unaware that the possession of good communication skills plays a large part in their selection to the prestigious colleges on which their hearts are set. They need to know, before it is too late, that the ability to speak well and write well will put them over and above other contenders every time in their chosen pursuits.

This is not an attempt to deal with accents or dialects; but rather an attempt to help you who feel the need to use the language more efficiently. You will avoid the use of words that do not exist—even though you hear them in the most surprising places; you will use some simple rules to construct your sentences, and you will treat with impunity the widespread misuse of punctuation.

Anyone, regardless of age or station, who recognizes a personal need for improvement in these areas and is willing to fulfill that need, I extend a warm welcome to *Say What*.

As a trainer and in my effort to improve my students' communication skills, I have often been asked this question: "Why do you want me to change? This is how I speak. My friends understand me when I talk to them." To this I respond with another question: "At that important college interview or your next job interview, will you be talking with your friends, or will you be talking with people who have the power to make life-changing decisions for you, based on how you present yourselves?"

Usually, this is followed by a long pause then a change of facial expression that signals a gradual awakening to the truth. I am always heartened by this reaction. It is the other that bothers me: the frown, the pursed lips, followed by the inevitable rolling of the eyes. Yet, I have never been deterred by the latter.

Our exciting venture together within these pages is not to prepare you for your friends—though we would like to have them along, too. Instead, it is for the many opportunities you will have everyday to communicate with confidence and credibility. Use it when your communication skills are needed to help make decisions about the next steps in your education. Use it to boost your success in your career, whether it is new or already established. Use it for your own success in life.

This is for the potential you, regardless of your age. You are ready, poised to venture onto a new level of communication; but feel the need to do some important work before the launching.

The improvement process does not end with the launching, however. Continue the practice so that this new knowledge becomes a part of you; so that everything you say is said naturally and confidently. Your knowledge of the language will prove its worth over and over again—during college interviews, job interviews, in business meetings, at social gatherings—whenever you communicate.

Avoid those situations during which one poor word choice or grammatical error cancels the effect of every good thing you have already said or might subsequently say. Your opportunity to make a good impression was there within reach, but is now lost.

So bear with me; or better, join me as we continue onward from a point where some parents, in bewilderment, may have left off. And since we must "teach our children how to speak [and write]" dear parents, I need you to partner with me as well, as I highlight, discuss and attempt to correct some of the more glaring diversions from the straight and narrow that I have encountered.

As you go through these pages, you will be sure to find material that does not apply to you personally; yet you may have heard it or seen it somewhere. I ask you, please, pass on the good news and help to stop the carnage.

Janet Carmichael

1

The Teeth, the Lips, the Tip of the Tongue:

- The Importance of Good Articulation
- Some that Suffer in Silence
- Exercises
- Good Practice Makes Us Perfect

The Importance of Good Articulation

Articulation is the correct pronunciation of every syllable of a word so that there is clarity and understanding when we speak. Good articulation is the very essence of good communication. When we articulate well, our sounds, syllables, and words are clearly formed and distinctly heard as the tongue, jaw, teeth, lips, and palate –all organs of articulation—work together to change the stream of air that leaves our lungs and impinges on our vocal cords. It follows then, that if we are to be clearly understood when we speak, we need to breathe well, energize those articulatory organs, and get them moving for us—whether we are speaking on the phone or face-to-face with someone. In short, let us put effort into our speaking. We must not mumble.

Sometimes, the articulation problem is deep-seated and needs the help of a speech–language pathologist or other medical professional. However, when poor articulation is merely the result of failure to use the basic speech sounds through poor use of the organs of articulation, just a little effort, some diligence, and a burning desire to improve communication skills will resolve the problem every time.

At times, poor articulation of a word is the result of incorrect spelling of that word. We spell and write the word incorrectly, and, as a result, we pronounce the word incorrectly—exactly as we spell it.

One word that immediately comes to mind is **February.** How often have you seen that word deprived of its fourth letter? How often have you not heard and seen *Feb-u-ary* written when the word should be written *Feb-ru-ary?*

In an attempt to say some words correctly—especially polysyllabic words—we should examine them syllable by syllable. In my classes, we pronounce each syllable slowly in order to get it right. When all the syllables are articulated correctly, the complete word is pronounced slowly, syllable by syllable, and then at a normal pace several times. Group practice follows in order to overcome the difficulty and reinforce the correct pronunciation.

With so many shades of differences to encounter as one hops around the English-speaking world—differences such as the one in which Americans drop the initial aspirate sound *h* from *herb* and *homage,* while in Britain the *h* is heard in these words—one is often left to wonder what is the right thing to say. A good rule to follow is this one: "When in Rome, do as the Romans do." Remember also that the main objective is communication.

Some that Suffer in Silence

I say that these (and others) suffer in silence because I am sure if they had the ability to speak out against the total disregard some people have for the correct way to pronounce them, they would.

Ask–a-s-k

It is often difficult for some people to avoid saying *aks (axe)* instead of the correct *ask*. A young person I know who, in spite of his nine years, has the agility of tongue better associated with a well-honed politician, pronounces words like *wasps, enthusiastic necessarily*, and even *supercalifragilisticexpialidocious* with precision—every syllable in its right place. But when he tries to say *ask*, he says instead, *aks*. It is needless to say that he and I have had many discussions about this and have been working on it together. However, I recently had an "aha" moment about this. His father also says *aks*.

Correct, Respect, Project–Cor-rect, Re-spect, Pro-ject

These words—and others like them—often lose their final consonants when we speak. The final *t* suffers total rejection and the word ends on the *c* instead. Similarly, many initial consonants are lost to listeners during communication, and this creates a strain on the process.

What a difference it would make to communication if we all took the time to use both initial and final consonants of words—unless, of course, the language requires the sound to be silent as in the silent *h* in *honest* and silent *p* in *psychology*.

February--Feb-ru-ary

Too often the first *"r"* in this word is completely ignored, and what is heard is Feb-*u*-ary instead of Feb-***ru***-ary (Feb-roo-ary). There is little wonder, then, that so many people misspell this word.They spell the word incorrectly because they pronounce it incorrectly.

Fifth,Fifty–Fif-th,Fif-ty

These words are categorically *fif-th* and *fif-ty,* and not *fit, or fith* and certainly not *fi-ty.* However, because of usage, we now see Webster's Collegiate Dictionary deftly incorporating this new pronunciation of *fith* alongside the accepted *fif-th.*

This update is not found in the Oxford English Reference Dictionary (2003).

Library–Li-bra-ry

Why would anyone want to substitute the correct pronunciation of this elegant little word with *li-bery*? Yet we do hear *li-bery* in the most surprising places when it should be *li-bra-ry.*

Nuclear--Nu-cle-ar

Fortunately, the mispronunciation of this word is not wide-spread. Most people who have cause to use this word regularly are able to pronounce it correctly.

Particularly--Par-ti-cu-lar-ly

Some disastrous attempts to say this word correctly are often due to a—let's face it—lazy tongue. In many cases, the penultimate syllable (**lar**) is the problem. It mysteriously disappears. When people take the time to pronounce each and every syllable this word contains we notice an amazing difference.

Pronunciation--Pro-nun-ci-a-tion

Derived from the verb, "pro<u>noun</u>ce", there is often a tendency to change the *nun* in the second syllable to *noun.* Here too, the spelling of the word tends to suffer as a result of this mispronunciation.

Recognize--Re-cog-nize

Very often the *"g"* sound is not used in *"recognize",* and we hear just *"re-co-nize".*

Really, there is no reason to dwell on that *"g"* sound, but do show awareness of its presence in this word and let it be heard ever so lightly. It will make a difference to your delivery.

Suite or Suit

Use the pronunciation, *suite* (*sweet*) when the reference is to a set of your furniture or a set of rooms. But remember to use *suit* (*syoot* or *soot*) for the smart item of clothing you sometimes wear when you choose to dress to impress.

Example: I love my new teak dining room *suite.*

I'll wear my red *suit* to the office today.

With

There are times when we hear *wif* instead of *with.* The *th* sound is replaced by an *f* sound. We hear this in certain speech communities both within and outside of the United States.

Women--Wo-men

It is quite right to use the *o* sound when we say *wo-man.* However, the *o* in *wo-men* is different. The *o* here has a short *i* sound as in *win.* We say *wi-men,* although it is written—*women.*

This is one good reason we should not teach reading using only the phonic method. Other methods are needed since English is not a phonic language. If it were, then, according to George Bernard Shaw, g*hoti* would be pronounced *fish.*

The *gh* would be assigned the *f* sound heard in rou*gh*
o would have the *i* sound heard in women
ti will be *sh* as in atten*ti*on

As we consider the impact that poor articulation could have on our social, our educational, and our vocational status, we should all agree that our speech is an important part of who we are. Therefore, we must not allow the quality of our lives to be adversely affected by a speech inadequacy; especially one that we can easily fix by exerting a little effort.

Too often we forget the need to energize the lips, jaw, and the tongue in order to improve voice quality and pronunciation. Loose jaws, active lips and agile tongues are essential to good speech.

Exercises

Equip yourself with a small mirror to do this exercise. This will give you an opportunity to see just how interesting you look as you first attempt to overuse the organs of articulation; but at the same time, you will observe these important speech organs at work. Now then, where is your mirror? Let us start.

The Jaw

This exercise stretches the lower jaw to loosen the action there.

Imagine having to bite on a large stack of crackers piled one on top of the other. Move your jaws–especially your lower jaw—in order to perform this feat. Repeat this exercise several times. Crunch! Crunch! Crunch!

1. Over-emphasize the use of the jaw and slowly say the following sentence three times:

    Pam picks gorgeous flowers while walking in the park.

2. Next, repeat the sentence at a normal pace, remembering to loosen the action of your lower jaw. Let it drop naturally.

The Lips

This exercise encourages flexibility of the lips, without which, words become indistinct.

1. Put your teeth together and let the corners of your mouth stretch slightly up toward your ears. Hold that position.

2. Now, change the position of your mouth to an exaggerated *oo* by protruding the lips as far out as they will go. Avoid any stiffness in the upper lip if you can.

3. Repeat this several times.

4. Now, using the agility of the lips, say these lines from the nursery rhyme at a moderately fast rate:

   Wee Willie Winkie rides through the town.

5. Say it once more at a normal pace making as much use of those important articulators—the lips.

Practice the *p* sound

Use greater lip involvement to say the following:

Peter Piper picked a peck of pickled pepper.
A peck of pickled pepper Peter Piper picked.
If Peter Piper picked a peck of pickled pepper,
Where's the peck of pickled pepper Peter Piper picked?

Here's an opportunity to use jaws and lips in the same exercise. Say these lines first at a moderately fast rate, then at a normal rate.

Wee Willie Winkie rides through the town
Upstairs and downstairs in his nightgown.

The Tongue

How to use the tongue in the formation of some vowel sounds.

Say What?
Here's How You Can Say and Write it Better

First, try to establish the position of the tongue as you say different vowels. Have you thought of this before? The correct placement of the tongue makes a great difference in the way your words are pronounced. I know you will say, "I never had to think about this before, so why should I bother with it now? And my response is: "For no other reason but the fact that we seek knowledge and improvement every day and for as long as we are alive." So now, are you alive or dead? Then let's go.

1. Say *ah* three times. Where is your tongue? It should be lying flat in your mouth with the tip against your bottom front teeth. Try it.

2. Say ee three times. Where is your tongue this time? It should be humped in your mouth with the tip once again against your lower front teeth.

3. Say *oo* three times. Where is your tongue? It should be flat again with the tip against your bottom front teeth.

4. The next activity will show you the power of the tongue to change sound.

   (a) Hold your jaw steady using your right hand. Let there be no movement of your jaw.

   (b) Say *ah, ee, ah, ee, ah, ee* , using only the changing positions of your tongue, as I explained above. You will notice how clearly these two vowel sounds can be produced with just the action of the tongue.

The Tongue

How we use the tongue in the formation of some consonants.

1. With open mouth, stretch your tongue out as far as you can then pull it in again. Repeat this exercise three times.
2. Next, use the agility of your tongue to repeat this nonsense rhyme which, together with the other two following here, I have created for you, dear readers of my book. First, learn the words then clap the rhythm as you say them to a steady beat. Above all, enjoy them and have fun.

Larry sent the latter lass a little letter later,
Then Larry lost the little letter as he lingered later,
Since Larry lingered later and so lost the little letter,
Lax Larry never sent the latter lass that little letter.

Practice the *th* sound by extending the tip of the tongue between the teeth

Through thick and thin the Thompson thoroughbreds
Thronged the throstle, then threw the throttle.

While doing these exercises, do not allow the tongue to be lazy or feeble.

Here is an exercise, the last in this set, that I consider very important:
Ask: Practice saying *ask:* and then continue with the lines below:

The asker had asked me if askance was acceptable
I answered the asker, "Choose askance or askant."
The asker said askance was much more supportable
Then the asker looked askant at the line of askaris.

Good Practice Makes Us Perfect

With good practice and diligence, very soon you will see how easy it is for anyone to use these organs efficiently to attain fluency of speech and improve communication skills. Stop yourself each time there is a tendency to mumble or to slur your speech or to pay scant attention to the correct pronunciation of words you already know how to pronounce. Don't drift backward. Move forward.

Equip yourself with a small tape recorder and a notebook. Listen to yourself and record your progress in those areas you identify as being in need of improvement. Work diligently on them and soon you will find that you have added a real touch of eloquence to what you have to say. What is more, others will be more inclined to listen when you speak.

View this preparation, not as an attempt to instill a feeling of disloyalty to the speech patterns and sentence structures you may have used from early childhood; but as an attempt to point the way to effective communication, to make a suitable impression wherever you go, and to prepare you for life.

I am reminded of a young hopeful who arrived one day to interview for a position in sales. He was dressed for the part; he had the required credentials, but he lacked the confidence and the enthusiasm. This all became evident as he mumbled his way through the interview. You may not be interviewing for a sales position, but at any interview, you have automatically become a salesperson; and the product is you.

So, before an interview, dress yourself suitably—this is important—but once there, sit up and show a natural interest. Speak clearly, intelligently, and with the right amount of excitement in your voice. Don't overdo it, but, above all, never mumble your way through your interview. Instead, set those articulators free.

2

It is not bigotry to be certain
we are right; but it is bigotry to be
unable to imagine how we might
possibly have gone wrong.
G.K. Chesterton, essayist and
novelist (1874-1936)

Let's Wage a War on "Words"

- The Non-word
- Malapropisms
- Colloquialisms

Non-Words

The non-words that I have included are the words
which we hear, but would never find in a dictionary.
Actually, they seem to exist only in the minds of the
people who use them. Therefore, the only valid term I
can find for them is the Non-Word.

According to Merriam-Webster's Online Dictionary,
the non-word is one "that has no meaning, is not known
to exist, or is disapproved." Here are some of them:

~~Affidavid~~--Affidavit

An affidavit is a written statement confirmed by oath
for use as evidence in court, therefore, the name David
is misplaced in this particular word.

Incorrect: The bank manager asked me to sign an
~~affidavid~~ when I lost all my checks.

Correct: The bank manager asked me to sign an *affidavit* when I lost all my checks.

~~Aggreance~~—Agreement
Incorrect: He said he was in ~~aggreance~~ with the idea we put forward.
Correct: He said he was in *agreement* with the idea we put forward.

~~Antartic~~—Antartic
~~Artic~~—Arctic
Where did the naughty little *c* go?

These words with their relation to the South and North Polar Regions respectively need the important first *c* pronounced in order to make it really **c**old and right.

Instead, too many people say and write ~~Antartic~~ and ~~Artic~~, allowing the *c* to disappear completely.

Correct: The Arctic region is that area around the earth's North Pole.

~~Bidness~~—Business
There is really no need to change the *z* sound to a *d* sound. This is found in certain speech communities.
Correct: *Business* (pronounced *biz-ness*)

~~Cannidate~~—Candidate
In any election year, it might be difficult to associate some candidates with our favorite candy. Let us try it, anyhow—even if it is just to get the pronunciation of this word right.

Let us say *candy-date* instead of canny-date, but write *candidate.*
Correct: Candidate

If the pronunciation of this word is dialectal, then it is part of a people's culture and should be left alone.

~~Conversate~~—Converse

Very often the person using this non-word is blissfully unaware that it is indeed a non-word and might even argue as to its correctness.

Incorrect: He stood in the hall ~~conversating~~ with his friends.
Correct: He stood in the hall *conversing* with his friends.

~~Crisises~~—Crises

The plural of the word *crisis* is *crises* (pronounced *cri-seez*) and not *crisises*—as was heard on one of our local radio stations:

> **Incorrect**: *"Musharraf has had a number of ~~crisises~~."*
> **Correct**: *Musharraf has had a number of crises.*

The plural of the word *crisis* is formed in the same way that *basis*, *oasis* and *thesis* form their plurals: by changing the *i* in the last syllable to an *e*: *bases, oases, theses,* **crises.**

~~Determent~~—Deterrent

This is a recent and surprising discovery. Here is what I actually saw written:

> **Incorrect**: Do *not let this be a ~~determent~~ to your willingness to help in this venture.*
> **Correct:** Do *not let this be a deterrent to your willingness to help in this venture*.

I hope that by including it here, there will be a complete and immediate eradication of this non-word before it takes root somehow in the minds of our young people.

~~Irregardless~~—regardless

The word "irregardless" is found in both the *Webster Dictionary* and the *Oxford English Reference Dictionary* –*OERD*--with cautionary remarks in both volumes. *Webster* uses the term: *nonstand.* which means that it is disapproved by many but might have some currency in certain contexts. The *OERD,* on the other hand, labels it *US dialect, jocular.* Both these references recommend, *regardless,* which is, undoubtedly, a better word if you want to be taken seriously.

Incorrect: ~~Irregardless~~ of the howling wintry winds, John ran out into the dark night without a coat.
Correct: *Regardless* of the howling wintry winds, John ran out into the dark night without a coat.

~~Interpretate~~—Interpret

Throw it out, please. There is no word like interpretate. The word is *interpret.*
Correct: *In-ter-pret*

~~Old-timer's Disease~~—Alzheimer's-disease

In spite of a seemingly obvious association, we should use the correct term for this debilitating affliction.
Correct: *Alzheimer's disease*

~~Stratergy~~—Strategy

Although most people know the correct pronunciation of this word, our young people may be prone to accept its incorrect pronunciation when it comes, unfortunately, from a source they assume to be knowledgeable.
Correct: *Stra-te-gy*

Vehicle

This word, although it does not fit into this list, is worthy of mention. Do not pronounce the aspirate *[h]* in this word. It was a pleasure to hear one of my favorite radio announcers on our local NPR station pronounce this word the way it should be pronounced—as if the *h* had been dropped from the word: **Ve-i-kl**. However the adjective, vehicular retains the aspirate *h* sound, and we say ve-hi-cu-lar.

Yes. I do agree with what you are thinking. What a strange and wonderful language.

Malapropisms

A malapropism, according to the Oxford English Reference Dictionary (2003), is the use of a word in mistake for another that sounds similar.

Highly comical at times, this term is derivative of the character of Mrs. Malaprop from Sheridan's *The Rivals (1775)* and deals only with valid words.

Examples: "*She danced a flamingo*" instead of "She danced a flamenco."

There is also this one from the lady herself giving advice: "Try to forget this fellow. *Illiterate* him, I say, quite from your memory." She meant *obliterate.*

Prostrate—Prostate

This is a well-worn example of a malapropism.

If the discussion is not about lying face downward especially in submission, but a reference instead to the male mammalian gland surrounding the neck of the bladder, then the appropriate word is *prostate*, not *prostrate*. Remove the offending second *r* and say, for instance, "He has had *prostate* surgery."

Correct: *pros-tate*

Colloquialisms.

Colloquialisms are acceptable in informal conversation and are easily understood among persons living in a particular speech community. An outsider, unfamiliar with the speech patterns of certain parts of a country, could find it difficult at first to understand what is being communicated. Examples of colloquialisms that immediately come to mind are:

Ya'll for **you all**
fixin' to do something for **about to do something**
They have their place in situations of familiarity such as communication with friends; but may not be used in formal speech or writing.

A ways to go for *a way to go*
Incorrect: We still have **a ways to go** before we reach the school.
Correct: We still have *a way to go* before we reach the school.

Anyways—Anyway
Incorrect: *Anyways,* I will be there before eight tonight.
Correct: *Anyway,* I will be there before eight tonight.

English is a living language and, therefore, it changes over time. Words change their meanings and others get accepted after continued usage. Strange as it may seem, hundreds of years ago, when Shakespeare wrote, the word "fond" meant "foolish".

In this line from *A Midsummer Night's Dream,* as the good bard dallies with the wonder and silliness of young

love, we hear Helena, as she rushes into the woods with Demetrius, panting for breath:
"Oh I am out of breath in this fond chase."
Surely, Helena was not using the word *fond* as we use it today.

Review and Practice Time

1. Choose the right word:

1. After a number of forged checks had been posted to her account, the bank asked her to sign an _____. (affidavit, affidavid)

2. She is still _____ with her teacher. (conversating, conversing)

3. _____ of what you now say, it will be difficult for me to believe you again. (regardless, irregardless)

4. This global economic downturn is said to be one of the worse financial _____ within the last twenty-five years. (crises, crisises)

5. The mission of this association is to eliminate _____ disease through the advancement of research. (Alzheimer's, Old timer's)

3

> I believe that every English poet should read the English classics, [and] master the rules of grammar before he tries to break or bend them.
>
> Robert Graves, English poet and novelist (1895-1985)

Render Results with Rules:

- Grammar: A definition
- Grammar: Two Branches of Study
- The Sentence
- The Verb
- Subject and Predicate

In the study of any language, one's knowledge of the rules of its grammar is germane to one's understanding of that language and using it well. It is, therefore, with some concern that we should look at the trend in our schools today to pay scant or no attention to the actual teaching of grammar. It is also little wonder that some students find it difficult to master the grammar of another language. How can they, when they have not yet learned the grammar of their own language?

Grammar: A definition

According to the *Oxford English Reference Dictionary,* (2003), grammar is the branch of language study [or linguistics] which deals with showing the relation of words as they are used in speech or writing. Grammar is based on a set of rules. In order to speak and write grammatically correct, one must be acquainted with these rules.

No sportsperson goes in to play a game without knowing the rules of the game. Then why should we attempt to communicate in any language without a knowledge of the rules of that language. Even more shocking is the fact that every effort is being made to keep our young students in the institutions of learning continuously clueless in this regard. They must learn the rules of the language.

Grammar: Two Branches of Study

1. **Syntax or sentence structure:** A study of the correct arrangement of words in a sentence and their relationship to one another.

2. **Morphology or Inflection:** A study of the way a word changes to show a difference in tense, number, gender. Do we need to know the terms syntax, inflexion, morphology? Not necessarily; but it is good to know that these words exist and what they mean.

The Sentence: A complete thought expressed in words.

It is as simple as this: We think and then we express our thoughts in writing or in speech. If the expressed thought is not complete, then it not a sentence. In order to qualify as a sentence, the thought expressed must be complete.

The Oxford Dictionary goes further with its definition of the sentence:

a set of words complete in itself as the expression of a thought, containing or implying a subject and predicate and conveying a statement, a question, exclamation or a command.

Webster's Ninth New Collegiate Dictionary goes even further in its definition:

a grammatically self-contained speech unit consisting of a word or a syntactically related group of words that expresses an assertion, a question, a command, a wish or an exclamation [which] in writing usually begins with a capital letter and concludes with appropriate end punctuation.

Statement or Assertion: *Little Bo-Peep has lost her sheep. I ate the cherries yesterday.*

Question: *Have you bought a new car?*

Exclamation: *Jump!* In this case, one word makes the sentence. The subject, "You", is implied or understood.

Command: *Put the rug on the floor.* Here again, the subject, "You", is understood.

Wish: *If only I were as tall as you are.* This construction is an example of the subjunctive mood—a later study.

Subject and Predicate

Remember: The sentence begins as a thought. We think it and then we say it or we write it. However, in order for our sentences to make sense, they must follow a grammatical sequence.

To better understand this, we will divide sentences into two large sections: a *subject* and a *predicate*. But in order to do this successfully, we must first identify the verb in the sentence.

The Verb is the action word

The verb is a very important part of every sentence, because it helps to give us the answer to a number of questions.

- Who or what performed the action—the Subject of the sentence
- To whom or to what was the action done—the Object of the sentence
- How, when, why or where the action was done—the Extension of the Verb.

As you can see, everything seems to hinge on the action in the sentence—the verb.

So, first things first: Let's find the verb.

The Subject
Here is a sentence:

Subject Verb   Object   Extension
Jack kicked the ball over the wall.

Ask the question: "Who or What *kicked* the ball?"
The answer is the subject of the sentence, *Jack*.
Always ask these **"who"** or **"what"** questions to find the subject of the verb which is also the subject of the sentence. **"Who"** indicates that the subject is a person or persons.

Here is another sentence:

Subject	verb	object	Extension

The heavy rain stopped the game today.

Ask the question: "What *stopped* the game?"

The answer is the subject of the sentence, *the heavy rain.*

Review and Practice Time

Ask the question to find the subject.
1. Little Bo-Peep *has lost* her sheep.
2. I *ate the cherries yesterday.*
3. Jump!

The answer, which is the subject, is in italics.

Who <u>has lost</u> (her sheep)? *Little Bo-Peep*
Who <u>ate</u> (the cherries)?   *I*
Who should <u>jump</u>? [*You.*] (The subject here is understood or implied.)

1. **Find the subject of each of these sentences and write them in the blanks below.**
   1. Jack and Jill went up the hill.
   2. Rylie and Ayden practice their steps every day.
   3. Kailey *understands* graphs well.
   4. The white cat *is sleeping* on my bed.
   5. Run!
   6. My family *loves* me.

Question	**Subject**
Who <u>went</u> (up the hill?)	_____
Who <u>practice</u> (every day?)	_____
Who <u>understands</u>?	_____
What <u>is sleeping</u> (on my bed)?	_____
Who <u>should run</u>?	_____
Who <u>loves</u> (me)?	_____

The Predicate

The Predicate contains everything that is said about the Subject; starting with the verb. To find the **predicate**, ask the question, "What was said about the subject?"

The answer is the predicate (in italics).

What is said about little Bo-peep? (Little Bo-peep) *has lost her sheep.*
What was said about me? (I) *ate the cherries yesterday.*

2. **Divide these sentences into Subject and Predicate.** The first two are done for you. **Start at #3.**
   1. Little Bo-Peep <u>has lost</u> her sheep.
   2. I <u>ate</u> the cherries yesterday.
   3. <u>Jump</u>!
   4. Jack and Jill <u>went</u> up the hill.
   5. Rylie and Ayden practice their steps every day.
   6. Kailey <u>*understands*</u> *graphs well.*
   7. The white cat <u>*is sleeping*</u> *on my bed.*
   8. My family <u>loves</u> me.

Say What?
Here's How You Can Say and Write it Better

Subject	Predicate
1. Little Bo-Peep	has lost her sheep
2. I	ate the cherries yesterday
3.	
4.	
5.	
6.	
7.	
8.	

4

Rules Still Rule the Roost

- The Object of the Verb
- Stop confusing "I" with "Me"
- The Extension of the Verb
- The Verb Revisited
- Function *vs* Position

Now that it is clear that the two large sections of a sentence are the Subject and Predicate, we can go a step further to see how the predicate can be further divided to show:

1. The Object of the Verb (or sentence) and
2. The Extension of the verb.

Here again, we see the verb in its role of guiding us to identify these important parts of the predicate.

The Object of the Verb

First, find the verb in the sentence, and then find the object of the verb by asking **"whom"** or **"what"** questions. The answer, in each case, will be the object of the verb.

Say What?
Here's How You Can Say and Write it Better

Subject Verb   Object   Extension (place)

Example 1. **Jenny found Dave at the top of the ladder.**

In this case we'll ask a **"whom"** question because the answer is a person—Dave. The question is: "*Whom* did Jenny find?" The answer is *Dave.* Dave is the object.

Subject Verb   Object   Extension (Place)

Example 2. **Jack kicked the ball over the wall.**

Ask the question, "*What* did Jack kick? The answer is *the ball. The ball,* is the object of the verb (or the sentence).

Subject   Verb   Object   Extension (time)

Example 3. **The heavy rain stopped the game today.**

Subject   Verb Object   Extension (manner)

Example 4. **The children greeted their parents with joy.**

Stop Confusing Me with I: We are not the same

The pronoun "**I**" is always, yes, **always** the subject of a sentence. The pronoun, "**I**", is always the doer of the action while the pronoun, "**me**" must forever be the object of the sentence. Imagine someone saying to you: *Kailey brought flowers for I.* You would immediately want to ask, "Why are you speaking in that strange way?"

You would never say, "Kailey *brought flowers for I.*"
Then why do so many people say and accept the following
incorrect sentence structures:

1. Kailey <u>brought</u> flowers for ~~Vanessa and I.~~(Incorrect)
2. Faith <u>sang</u> a song for ~~Pat and I.~~ (Incorrect)
3. The children <u>like</u> their ~~teacher and I.~~ (Incorrect)
4. Shaun <u>called</u> ~~Pat and I~~ after the game. (Incorrect)

> The verbs are under-lined for you. Try this:
> Delete the **person's name** that follows the verb. Now, delete the word "**and**" that follows that name. Notice carefully what is left. It is something that you would never say.

The sentences above are all hopelessly wrong; yet
we hear them every day.

Why are they wrong? They are wrong because too
many people delight in confusing these two pronouns: *I*
and *me.* Whenever you find the pronoun, *I,* in a sentence,
you can be sure it is doing something to someone. It is
never on the receiving end of the action.

Remember: The pronoun I is always the <u>subject</u> of
a verb—the doer of an action. It is never the receiver
of an action and, therefore, never the <u>object</u> (or, for that
matter, the indirect object) of the verb. The pronoun, *me,*
however, is always the object, the receiver of the action.
So let us correct the sentences:

          Direct Object   Indirect Object

1. Kailey brought flowers for Vanessa and me. (Correct)

          Dir. Object   Indirect Object

2. Faith sang a song for Karen and me. (Correct)

Direct   Object

3. The children like their teachers and me. (Correct)

Direct Object

4. Shaun called Pat and me after the game. (Correct)

The Direct and Indirect Object

It is easy to tell the difference between the Direct Object and the Indirect Object.

The Direct Object <u>directly</u> answers the "whom" and "what" questions.

The Indirect Object comes after a preposition, and answers the questions: "for whom?" or "for what"? "with whom?" or "with what?"

Kailey brought flowers for Vanessa and me.

In this sentence we ask the question, "What did Kailey bring?" The answer is "flowers for Vanessa and me." the complete object.

But what did Kailey actually bring in her hand to give to us? The answer, the **direct** answer is **flowers.** Therefore the noun, *flowers,* is the **direct object.**

However, we cannot simply ignore the other words that make up the complete object and which have been included to tell us **for whom** the flowers were brought. So we ask the question, "For whom did Kailey bring the flowers? The answer, *Vanessa and me,* is the **indirect object.**

Roy bought Karen a beautiful guitar when she was sixteen years old.

"What did Roy buy?" The answer, *a beautiful guitar,* is the **direct object**. Now, ask the question, "For whom did Roy buy the guitar?" The answer, *Karen*, is the **indirect object**.

Between you and me
The often-heard *between you and I* is incorrect. Say *between you and me.* See how the preposition "between" precedes *you and me*. Remember that the subject pronouns such as. *I, she, he, we, they* never trail after a preposition. Never! They are too busy **doing** things, performing actions.

Function *vs*. Position
It is not necessarily where the word is placed in the sentence, but rather how the word functions in the sentence that matters. Here is a construction that needs to be guarded against: By the way, it is not a grammatical crime to end a sentence with a preposition as I just did. There are times when it cannot be avoided.

Incorrect: John is shorter than ~~me~~.
Correct: John is shorter than I.

Without applying the rules, one may argue that since the pronoun, *me* is at the end of this construction, then it is correct. But it is not. Remember we look at function, and not the position of the word in the sentence.

John is shorter than I means *John is shorter than I am.*

You would never say: *John is shorter than me am,* would you? *Therefore,* do not say: John is shorter than ~~me~~. Say and write, "John is shorter than I."

The Extension of the Verb

These were sneaked into some examples above when we dealt with Objects of the verb. I hope you noticed them. Just to reiterate, we find the Extension of the Verb when we again use the verb to ask:

1. **Where** did the action occur?" Extension of place
2. "**When** did the action occur?" Extension of time
3. "**How** did the action occur?" Extension of place.

1. **Where** did Jack kick the ball? Over the wall (Extension of _____)
2. **When** did the rain stop the game? Today (Extension of _____)
3. **How** did the children greet their parents? With joy (Extension of _____)

These, then, are the prime parts of the predicate: verb, object, and extension of the verb. When we set out the whole sentence in a table like the one below, we are analyzing the sentence; for our purpose, a simple sentence. Study this table. It will help you in the practice section later in this chapter.

Analysis of the Simple Sentence

Subject	Predicate		
	Verb	**Object**	**Extension**
Who? What?	Action	Whom, What	How? When? Where?
Jean	plays	the piano	well (manner)
Ryan	lost	his ring	yesterday (time).
Pat	drove	his new car	to work (place)
(You)	stop!		
Her family	loves	her	very much (manner)

The Verb Revisited

A recent issue of one of my favorite online newsletters, *A .Word. A. Day* with Anu Garg, had this to say about verbs:

"If verbs are, in fact, as conceited as Humpty-Dumpty claims them to be, perhaps they can be forgiven for their hoity-toity ways—after all, they are the ones that bring a sentence to life."

This was based on Humpty Dumpty's boast about words in Lewis Carol's 1872 classic, *Through the Looking Glass,*—but we will discuss more of that in the next chapter.

Do you agree that the verb is about **the most** important part of any sentence?

Say What?
Here's How You Can Say and Write it Better

Let's look at it this way: A simple sentence can survive without an expressed subject, as in sentence four above; but there can never be a simple sentence without an expressed verb.

Let's prove it: *The baby under the table.* This is a fragment, or a phrase. The verb is absent. Merely a group of words "forming a conceptual unit, but not a sentence" (OERD 2003), these words fail to make a complete thought.

Imagine someone saying this to you, "The baby under the table." Would you not be inclined to respond, "Yes? What about the baby? What did the baby <u>do</u> under the table?"

However, if we add a verb to show what the baby *does,* or what the baby *is doing,* or what the baby *did,* or even what the baby *will do,* then we will have a sentence—a *complete* thought. Look at the following sentences:

- The baby *creeps* under the table. (Simple present tense)
- The baby *is sitting* under the table (Present continuous tense)
- The baby *slept* under the table. (Past tense)
- The baby *will play* under the table. (Future tense)

I think we agree that the action word is absolutely necessary. Each of the sentences above now makes perfect sense.

Review and Practice Time

1. Insert *I* or *me* in the blanks below.

1. I bought pretty little key rings in Italy for my family and _____.
2. Karen waved to Gayle and _____ as we boarded the 'plane.
3. Tom, Dick, Harry and _____ quickly ran to the door.
4. Shaun is taller than _____.
5. They brought several books for Riley and _____.
6. He arrived at the meeting later than _____
7. Terry and _____ sang a duet at the concert.

2. Identify the direct and indirect object in each sentence.

1. Cherie brought doughnuts for her sister and me.
   a. Direct Object: _____
   b. Indirect Object: _____

2. Ayden bought his mother a beautiful ring.
   a. Direct Object: _____
   b. Indirect Object: _____

3. Analyze the following simple sentences using the table below.

1. The children were playing in the park yesterday.
2. Every week I put fresh flowers in my vases.
3. The little girl and her mother ran quickly up the stairs.
4. After the concert, we went to a restaurant.

Remember: First, find the verb, and then ask the questions to find the subject, object and extension of the verb.

Subject	Predicate		
	Verb	Object	Extension

With these exercises completed, I can hear you asking yourself, "What is 'all this' about? Why do I need to be bothered with this?"

Try not to view it as a bother, but as a means of seeing for yourself how "all this" fits into the whole business of word relationships within a sentence and how this knowledge will help you to better understand the mechanics, as it were, behind correct sentence construction.

Take the time to analyze the sentence. Observe how each word functions in the sentence. Then soon and very soon, you will know when and why a word is out of place and be able, on your own, to make the necessary corrections to all you say and write. No longer will you wonder whether the structure of your sentence is right or wrong. No longer will there be a need to enter into a guessing game. You will know immediately because you have practiced it.

In the next few pages, be prepared to see how the incorrect placing of the subject pronoun *I* in the object of a sentence always results in a poorly constructed sentence. Yet people do it all the time.

We should never throw words into a sentence allowing them to fall wherever they will. Instead, we must carefully place words based on their function, on their relationship with other words in the sentence, keeping always within grammatical guidelines.

In order to do this well—as in any game we play, and as with life itself—we need to know and follow the rules. Play the game with a sound knowledge of the rules and there is a strong chance you will win. Even if you don't win, you will have played a great game.

5

Words Need a Relationship

- The Parts of Speech
- Why Words Change
- How Tense Changes Words
- How Number Changes Words
- The Verb "to be"
- There is and There are

We use words to convey our thoughts and in order to do that well, words need other words to work with them in establishing a good relationship within a sentence; words that work together to protect the grammatical integrity of what we say and write. This brings us to the point where we need to revisit the parts of speech you studied a long time ago and for which you now swear you have no earthly use. Perhaps, you are right; but just humor me. We won't interest ourselves here with definite and indefinite articles (the, a and an). At this time we are concerned only with the parts of speech.

They are only eight of them, eight parts of speech, eight categories of words, but as I mentioned earlier, Humpty Dumpty from Lewis Carol's *Through a Looking*

Glass thinks all words have a temper, especially verbs. Let's see.

The Parts of Speech

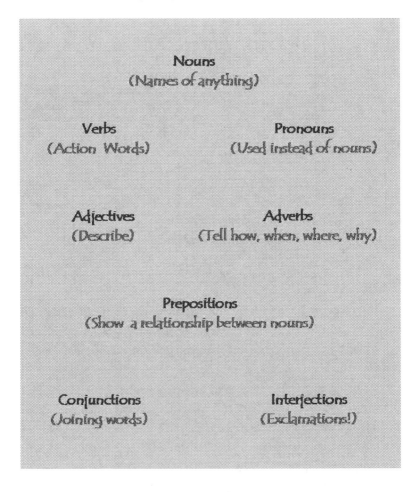

Nouns
(Names of anything)

Verbs
(Action Words)

Pronouns
(Used instead of nouns)

Adjectives
(Describe)

Adverbs
(Tell how, when, where, why)

Prepositions
(Show a relationship between nouns)

Conjunctions
(Joining words)

Interjections
(Exclamations!)

The Part of Speech, as was mentioned before, is the category to which a word is assigned. These categories are based on the function of a word in a sentence. However, even as words are assigned to these different categories, in each sentence, they maintain a relationship with one another. They depend on one another to make sense of what we say—both logically and grammatically. For instance, if you use an adjective in place of an adverb, you will end up with a badly constructed sentence.

Here is an example of this that I see on signs prominently placed in areas frequented by young children attending school.

Drive ~~slow~~. Children at play.

My first concern is for the dear, little ones who are offered this daily serving of poor grammar. At what point will they come to realize that *slow* is an adjective and should not be used when you are telling someone **how** to do something—as only an adverb should. Certainly, someone had to order that sign and pay for it. Surely, that sign should read:

Drive slowly. Children at play.

Here is another: *She sang that song really ~~good~~.*

Good is an adjective. It *describes* a noun. The word, *good,* does no describing in this sentence. Instead we need a word here that tells *how* she sang. Let's use *well,* an adverb. Let's make the change and see the difference here:

She sang that song really well.

The ability to
1. Identify the Part of Speech of a word
2. Describe that word's function in a particular sentence, and
3. Show how the word relates to other words in the same sentence, are all requirements in a grammatical process known as parsing.

The word to be parsed is always presented as part of a sentence—a necessity if we are to see the function of the word under consideration. The function is based on the work the word does in that particular sentence—in the particular context. As we know well, the same word could perform different functions in different sentences.

Example 1 shows the same word, **bowl,** with different meanings in two sentences:
• The ladies *bowl* at the local rink every evening. (verb)
• She had a small *bowl* of soup for lunch. (noun)

Example 2 shows the same word, **smell,** with the same meaning.
• I *smell* the lovely fragrance of roses in the air. (verb)
• The *smell* of freshly-baked bread greeted us as we entered the house. (noun)

Parsing is an exercise that works hand-in-hand with sentence analysis. Long ago, schools used to teach this in English Language classes. They stopped when the entire teaching profession was exposed to, and duly caught the anti-grammar disease. I do not blame the teaching profession. I blame instead the people who are responsible for making education policy, which is, in turn, handed down to the teaching profession to implement..

Parsing has its merits. When words in a sentence are examined, given their function and relationship to other parts of the sentence on a regular basis, the students who do these exercises everyday will soon learn the mechanics of the language, and this can only lead to more efficient use of the language. Students will come to recognize faulty sentence structures all on their own. This made a lot of sense. It made so much sense that the practice of teaching parsing and sentence analysis seems to have become redundant.

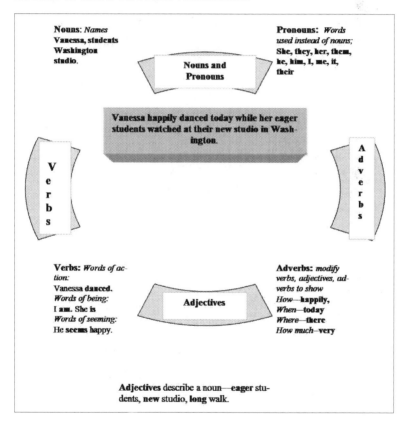

Nouns: *Names*
Vanessa, students
Washington
studio.

Nouns and Pronouns

Pronouns: *Words used instead of nouns;* **She, they, her, them, he, him, I, me, it, their**

Vanessa happily danced today while her eager students watched at their new studio in Washington.

V e r b s

A d v e r b s

Verbs: *Words of action:*
Vanessa danced.
Words of being:
I am. She is
Words of seeming:
He seems happy.

Adjectives

Adverbs: *modify verbs, adjectives, adverbs to show* **How—happily,** *When*—**today** *Where*—**there** *How much*—**very**

Adjectives describe a noun—**eager** students, **new** studio, **long** walk.

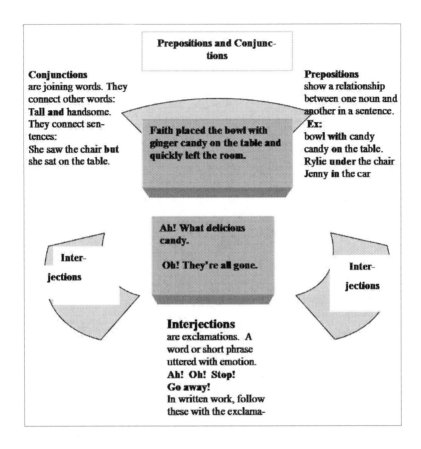

Prepositions and Conjunctions

Conjunctions
are joining words. They
connect other words:
Tall **and** handsome.
They connect sentences:
She saw the chair **but**
she sat on the table.

Faith placed the bowl with
ginger candy on the table and
quickly left the room.

Prepositions
show a relationship
between one noun and
another in a sentence.
Ex:
bowl with candy
candy on the table.
Rylie under the chair
Jenny in the car

Ah! What delicious
candy.

Oh! They're all gone.

**Inter-
jections**

**Inter-
jections**

Interjections
are exclamations. A
word or short phrase
uttered with emotion.
Ah! Oh! Stop!
Go away!
In written work, follow
these with the exclama-

The Preposition

Harking back to the earlier mention of the real frenzy some people get into if they hear a preposition placed at the end of a sentence, I can call on no better authority than Winston Churchill who once said, with dry humor, I am sure:

"From now on, ending a sentence with a preposition is something up with which I will not put."
Winston Churchill, British politician, Nobel Prize winning author and statesman *(1874-1965)*

Why Words Change

Many of us are at ease with the way a word changes to show a difference in tense, for instance, because we have used them all your lives. Imagine, however, the difficulty that others who are now learning English would have with these changes.

The study of inflexion (**morphology**) deals with the way words change to show a difference in:

(1) Tense (verbs)—walk, walked, have walked; come, came, have come.

(2) Gender (nouns, pronouns)—heir, heiress;   boy, girl;   he, she;   him, her;

(3) Number (nouns, pronouns and verbs)

For our purpose, we will concentrate on **Tense** and **Number** since more grammatical errors in speech and writing are made with the incorrect use of tense and number.

Tense
How Tense Changes Words

The present tense and the past tense cause few problems in regular verbs. Regular verbs just add an *ed* to the present tense to form the past tense.

Present	past	present	past
Example: walk,	walked;	talk,	talked.

Irregular verbs, however, are not as simple as this. They behave in strangely different ways to form the past tense.

Present	past	present	past
Example: come,	came;	go,	went.

The Past Participle

When some attempt to use the past participle, there are even more problems. The past participle indicates that an action has been completed at a time more distant than the immediate past.

It is formed with *has, have* (or *had)* together with a form of the verb. Sometimes the form of the verb used for the past participle is *the past tense,* in other cases, it is not. There is no rule that points you to the right form of the verb to use in each case. This just has to be learned.

Let us examine the present, past and past participle of the verb "to bring":

I bring, I brought, *I have brought*.

Here we use the past tense of the verb to form the past participle. Remember with some verbs it not as easy. For instance:

Incorrect: You sing, you sang, you *have ~~sang~~.*
Correct: You sing, you sang, you *have sung.*

I learn. I learned. I have learned.

He learns. He learned. He *has learned.*

(In other parts of the English speaking world, *learnt* is used instead of *learned.*)

Here are some other examples of the way verbs change.

Present Tense	Past Tense	Past Participle
The apples *fall* from the tree every day.	The apples *fell* from the tree yesterday.	The apples *have fallen* from the tree. They are all on the ground.
I do	I did	I have done, I had done
I fly	I flew	I have flown, I had flown
I eat	I ate	I have eaten, I had eaten
I drive	I drove	I have driven, I had driven
I think	I thought	I have thought, I had thought
I know	I knew	I have known, I had known

Number
How Number Changes Words

In the English language, number affects nouns, pronouns and verbs.

Singular number—one
Plural number—more than one

The **child** *talks* loudly. (Singular) The **children** *talk* loudly. (Plural)

He *prefers* to drive *his* own *car.* (Singular) **They** *prefer* to drive *their* own *cars.* (Plural)

A rule to remember: The verb must agree with its subject in number.

The athlete sprints to the finishing line. In this sentence, the **singular verb**, *sprints*, agrees with its **singular subject,** *athlete.*

The athletes sprint to the finishing line. In this sentence, the **plural verb**, *sprint,* agrees with its **plural subject,** athletes.

An Interesting Conclusion

One day, during a training session, after spending some time trying to get this concept understood, there were still a few puzzled faces, so I decided to divide the class into two groups and play a game.

In the game I directed a sentence to each group, leaving out the verb. The group with the first correct answer won two points and gained one contestant from the losing side. The winning group would be the one that ends the game with the higher number of points and the larger intake of members from the other side. It was rapid, energetic and a lot of fun. At the end of the exercise, I suggested they take some time for discussion, which they gladly did.

After a while, someone in one of the groups said quite loudly, "Ah! We understand it now. One gets two and two get one." In utter disbelief, I said, "What?" But in chorus they responded. "Yes! One gets two and two get one." All this was said with the greatest emphasis on the words affected. (one gets; two get) This took me some time to digest; but after a while, I realized what they were talking about.

They had decided that, since, in many cases, an **s** on the **plural noun** is followed by no **s** on **its plural verb**; and no **s** on the **singular noun** is followed by an **s** on the **singular verb,** then it follows that one gets two and two get one. That was their way of dealing with the problem they saw.

The girl plays in the park.
The girls play in the park.

Amusing as it was at the time, I had to warn them to be cautious with their new findings.

Note: The **subject pronouns, *I* and *you* always take a plural verb.**

The Verb "To be"

Although this work does not necessarily require us to move into a spiritual realm, I found this quote much too compelling to resist.

> Most people spend their lives trying to conjugate the verbs "to want', "to have", and "to keep" . . . when all the Spirit wills us to do is to conjugate the verb, "to be".
> —Evelyn Underhill, English writer, pioneer of ecumenism, peace and social justice. (1875-1941)

It also helps, in an interesting way, to reveal the true meaning of the verb "to be".

The verb "to be" is one of the most widely used verbs in the English language, and takes many different forms. In most cases, the verb "to be" does not indicate an <u>action</u> on the part of its subject, but rather a sense of <u>being</u>, a state of existence.

Example: *I* <u>am</u> *happy. You* <u>are</u> *here.*

It is only when it serves as an auxiliary, helping another verb to form the finite verb that the verb "to be" finds itself involved in real action.

Example: I <u>am running</u>. You <u>are jumping</u>.

Here are the very basic forms of the verb "to be" in singular and plural forms and also in past and present tenses:

am, is, was—are, were

The verb "to be" has a strange way of using the same CASE before it as after it. It is as though these sentences have two subjects. Although not quite as simplistic, this rule requires that we use the **subject** pronoun, *I,* instead of the object pronoun, *me* in certain sentence constructions. At first glance this may seem quite wrong, but it is right. Here is one of these constructions.

Incorrect: The trainers in this facility are Patrick and me.

Since the pronoun, *me,* placed at the end of this sentence gives us a construction which we must avoid, let's get it right.

...........Subject......................   Verb

Correct: The trainers in this facility are Patrick and I.

Look at the sentence a little closer and you will see the logic. There really is no action. The verb "to be" indicates no action, no transference of action from a subject to an object. The sentence just describes the way things are. If we were to flip the sentence around like this:

...... Subject......Verb

Patrick and I are the trainers in this facility, it will lose none of its meaning and you will immediately understand why the first sentence was faulty.

We see here once again, that it is not the position of the word, but the function of the word in the sentence that matters. What is more, I am sure **y**ou would never say, "Patrick and me are the trainers in this facility."

Remember:
* The verb "*to be*" takes the same case before it as after it.
* The subject of a sentence is always the Nominative Case. Therefore, the pronoun that follows the verb "*to be*" must also be *the Nominative Case* and not the *Objective Case*.

This is good information to have, even though we will not study Case here.

If a caller on the telephone says, "May I speak with Janet, please?" I respond, "This is she." Although this is grammatically correct, you know as well as I do, that some people prefer to say anything else but "This is she" or "This is he."

Example2: We use it with *suppose* to help in forming the verb in some sentences, but often it is used here incorrectly. Very often you hear, **I am suppose** instead of **I am supposed.**

Incorrect: I *am suppose* to be leaving tomorrow.

Correct: I *am supposed* to be leaving tomorrow.

"There is" and "There are" as we begin a sentence

Whenever we begin a sentence with "*There is*", we must follow with a singular subject and, likewise, "*There are*" should be followed by a plural subject. This is what is called (I was about to say a "no-brainer", but I cannot encourage slang within these pages, so let me start again.) This is something so easy and simple as to require no thought. (a Google definition). Yet over and over again, people use *"There is"* to begin a sentence and religiously follow with a plural subject. It is rampant on the airwaves and on television programs, and every time I hear it, I cringe.

Example:
Incorrect: ~~There is~~ a few people <u>standing</u> in the hall.
Correct: There <u>are</u> a few people <u>standing</u> in the hall.

There is begins a sentence when the subject following is singular.

Incorrect: ~~There is~~ sixteen bottles <u>hanging</u> on the wall. (Verb underlined.)
Correct: There <u>are</u> sixteen bottles <u>hanging</u> on the wall.

The incorrect sentence has a plural subject, *sixteen bottles*, that follow a singular verb: *is standing*. We never do that. The rule says:

The verb must agree with its subject in number.

If the subject is singular, begin the sentence with *There is*. which is also singular.
If the subject is plural, begin with *There are*. It is as simple as that. Therefore, it baffles me when people blatantly mess up this construction.
A note of warning, however: Be ever mindful of constructions like the following:
There is a group of people standing in the hall.

Here the question arises, "Should we use "t*here is*" or "t*here are*"? The subject here is **a group**, even though *of people* is also part of the subject, these words only qualify the subject word, *group*. Since it is **one group**, then the subject is **singular.** Use *there is.*

In the sentence following, we will use *"There are"* as we now have a plural subject: *two groups.*

> *There are two groups of people standing in the hall.*
> *(Two groups of people are standing in the hall.)*

I once overheard this exchange on a local radio program:

Interviewer: Are there any plans to make it better?

Interviewee: Certainly, ~~there is~~ plans to make it better.

If you were to spin that sentence around, you would realize that the interviewee was saying: Certainly~~, plans is~~ there to make it better.

No one says that. Then why do people use the same wrong construction over and over again?

Correct: Certainly, there are plans to make it better.

The prevalence of this faulty construction fills me with a despair that one day soon it will be deemed the correct thing to say, for, as we know so well, such is the behavior of a language as alive and vibrant as English is. However, for the present, let us say and write the correct thing with the hope that sanity will prevail.

Review and Practice Time

1. **Fill the blanks with the correct tense of the verb to know based on the meaning of the sentence.**

   1. He _____ that his sister **has** a pony.
   2. He _____ that his sister **had** a pony.
   3. He _____ _____ for some time that his sister **had** a pony.

2. **Incorrect**: She ~~do~~ the dishes.
   Correct: She _____ the dishes.

3. **Fill the blanks with the correct past participle using the verb indicated:**

   1. I _____ _____ my exercises for the day. (to do)
   2. John _____ _____ to the movies. He's not at home. (to go)
   3. Terry _____ _____ to see you; but you had already left. (to come)
   4. The boys _____ _____ this song before. (to sing)

4. **Fill the blanks, using these verbs: write writes; walk, walks.**

   1. She _____ messages every day.
   2. They _____ messages before leaving for school.
   3. He _____ to the city every day
   4. They _____ to the city each morning

5. **Fill the blanks with *there is* or *there are*.**

   1. _____ _____ a beautiful bunch of roses in the vase.
   2. _____ _____ a few people waiting for the bus.
   3. _____ _____ many reasons why our team should have won.

4. _____ _____ over fifty children playing in the park today.

5. _____ _____ a large number of dry leaves on the front lawn.

6. Choose the right pronoun after the verb "to be":

1. The only singers here <u>are</u> you and (me, I).
2. The last to leave the classroom <u>will be</u> Carol and (I, me).
3. The angels in the play were Faith and (me, I).
4. The two teachers present today <u>are</u> Shaun and (me, I).

7. Can you identify the eight parts of speech in these sentences?

1. We saw the young lady in the red dress walk slowly across the patio.
2. The old man rested after the long walk.
3. The children applauded loudly as the clowns entered the stage at the circus.
4. They always exercise before breakfast.

5. "Ah!" she exclaimed, "There you are."
6. Before the game, the players quickly kick the ball over the high fence.
7. The first kick sent the ball into the stands.
8. Meg has completed the exercise she had for homework.

Nouns	Pronouns	Verbs	Adjectives	Adverbs	Prepositions	Conjunctions	Interjections

6

> I believe that we are solely re-
> sponsible for our choices, and we
> have to accept the consequences
> of every deed, word, and thought
> throughout our lifetime.
> —Elisabeth Kubler-Ross
> author and psychiatrist. (1926-2004)

A Choice of Words:

- A and An
- Amount and Number
- Center on not center ~~around~~
- Comprises not ~~is comprised of~~
- Different from not different ~~than~~
- In regard, to; with regard to not **in ~~regards~~ to,
  with ~~regards~~ to**
- Who and Whom
- Why **Lie** and **Lay** Cause Trouble
- **Their** after the antecedent

What a challenge it is sometimes to choose the right word. So often we are confronted with two words, sometimes similar to each other; but having been exposed far too long to the incorrect choice, that is the one chosen without a second thought. Should someone dare to offer a correction, often the reaction is: "But that doesn't sound right." It does not, because your ear has become so conditioned to the incorrect thing that the correct choice now sounds wrong. Here are a few words that require your ability to make the right choices.

Choose with Care

A and An

The fact that these two little words confuse some people continues to be a mystery.

Rule: **An**: a form of the indefinite article is used before words beginning with a vowel sound (**an** apple, **an** honest man). Before words beginning with a consonant sound, use the indefinite article **a** (a cat, a mouse, a bird).

Incorrect: It only took me ~~a~~ hour to get here.
Correct: It took me *an hour* to get here.

Incorrect: He is ~~a~~ *honest* man.
Correct: He is *an honest* man.

Here are other examples of the correct use of *a* and *an:*
I ate an apple and an orange at lunch today.
This is *an opportunity* I would not miss.
I found *a hotel* near the airport.

Interestingly, although it is acceptable to say *a history book*, people rarely say *a historical novel*. Instead, most people say *an historical novel*.

Amount and Number

I have devised a simple way to get students to use these two words with some accuracy. Use **number** instead of **amount** whenever the discussion is about something that can be counted. For instance, say: *At breakfast this morning, I ate a large **number** of strawberries and a small **amount** of cereal.* Try switching places with *number* and *amount* in this sentence and you'll see that at least it works here.

Center on not Center~~around~~

Incorrect: Our discussion today will *center ~~around~~* the importance of using good language.

Correct: Our discussion today will *center on* the importance of using good language.

Let us see how the example above well demonstrates how more accurate is the choice of **center on** than **center around**: Since the center is a focal point, we can only center *on* a point; never *around* a point. Of course, that assumes we want to see progress.

Comprises or is composed of—not ~~comprises of~~

Incorrect: The team is ~~comprised of~~ three senators and five congressmen

Correct: The team **comprises** three senators and five congressmen.

The team **is composed of** three senators and five congressmen.

The preposition **of** should not immediately follow any form of the word **comprise**.

Different from not different ~~than~~

Correct: The hat she wore today is **different from** the one she wore yesterday.

Incorrect: The hat she wore today is **different ~~than~~** the one she wore yesterday.

We can say that one thing differs *from* the other. We never say one thing differs than the other. So why say something is *different than* another?

Who and Whom

Rarely does one hear the use of the word "whom". The favorite is "who" regardless of the word's function in the sentence. *Who* and *Whom* are two relative pronouns. Let's see how they function. The pronoun, *who*, always refers to the subject of the verb, while the pronoun, *whom,* refers to the object of the verb.

Remember: A pronoun is a word used instead of a noun.

So, here is a sentence: *Vanessa* loves *Ayden.*

Let us substitute [Who] and [Whom] for the two proper nouns, Vanessa and Ayden. *Who* loves *whom?* Immediately, it is clear that *who* represents the subject, Vanessa, The Nominative Case, while *whom* represents the object, *Ayden*—the Objective Case.

Vanessa performed the action while Ayden received the action. Now, if you ask the question, "Whom does Vanessa love?" you will be using **whom** correctly, since *whom* refers to Ayden in this sentence. Therefore, we should **not** say, "**Who** does Vanessa love?" since *who* can only refer here to the subject; in this case, Vanessa.

Paul <u>bought</u> this shirt. *Who* bought the shirt? Paul performed the action; therefore the word, *Paul* is the subject of the verb, **bought** and **who,** the subject pronoun, must be used when referring to Paul.

Many years ago, a university professor said to my then journalism-student daughter that the use of correct grammar is "a feminine thing". Naturally, I succumbed to a feeling of intense outrage for these reasons: First, that the importance of correct grammar should be so summarily dismissed and then, that anything feminine should be considered in a derogatory sense! I feel the anger surging even now as I recall.

Do not allow yourselves to drift into a state where you become oblivious to the rules of grammar. Instead, adhere to these simple rules. They will help, not hinder your progress.

Why Lay and Lie Cause Trouble

Be careful with these two; they are tricky. Before we study *lay* and *lie*, let me bore you a little about transitive and intransitive verbs. This explanation will open your eyes to all the secrecy surrounding the correct use of *lay* and *lie* and make them easy to understand. So here goes:

Transitive and Intransitive Verbs (To better understand lay and lie)

Definition: A **trans**itive verb is a verb that **trans**fers the action from a subject to an object.

Example1: *Rylie* (subject) <u>kicked</u> *the ball.*

What did Rylie kick? She kicked the ball. *The ball* is the object. (I know you remember this well.) But here is something new: The verb, *kicked*, is a transitive verb. Why is kicked transitive? The action was directly **trans**ferred from Rylie to the ball.

Example 2: The dog <u>ate</u> the bone.

The dog (subject) <u>ate</u> something. What did the dog eat? The dog <u>ate</u> *the bone.*

The bone is the object.

Therefore, the verb, ate, is a **trans**itive verb.

The Intransitive Verb

As the name implies, there is no transferring from subject to an object with these verbs. They are intransitive.

Example 1: The baby <u>cried</u> last night. No action passes from the subject, *baby*, to an object. In fact, there is no object. *Last night* is an extension of the verb showing **time** (when the baby cried).

Example 2: The radio <u>plays</u> loudly all day.

Again, in this sentence, the verb, *plays*, is an **intrans**itive verb. There is no transferred action to an object.

But let's change the sentence to:

The radio *plays* sweet music all day.

Immediately you will notice that the verb *plays* in this sentence is transitive. To prove this true, ask the question, "What does the radio play?" The answer *sweet music* is the object. This sentence has an object. The verb transfers the action from *the radio* to the *sweet music*. You can see the link between the two.

Conclusion: A transitive verb has an object; while an intransitive verb has no object. We are now ready to deal with *lay* and *lie*.

Lay is a <u>transitive verb</u> when it is in the <u>present tense</u>, meaning to put or place on a surface.

Object

Example 1: I *lay* <u>my keys</u> on the table every night. (Present tense)

Object

Example 2: My hens *lay* <u>large eggs</u>. (Present tense)

In these sentences, *lay* transfers the action from a subject to an object.

You may ask, "What do I lay?" and get the object of the verb *lay*—but only when *lay* is in the present tense. The past tense of **lay,** in this case, is **laid.**

Correct:
I *laid* my keys on the table last night.
Last year, my hens *laid* large eggs.

Lie is an intransitive verb, in the present tense. It means to assume a horizontal position on a supporting surface.

Lie does not transfer the action from subject to an object. You do not *lie* something on anything. There is no "**Lie what**?" There is no object after the verb, *lie*.

Example 1: It's time to go to sleep, Riley, Come and *lie* on your bed. (Present tense)

Example 2: The mechanic *lies* under the car. (Present tense)

Lay is an <u>intransitive verb</u> when it is the <u>past tense of lie</u>

Here again is the word *lay*; but this time, *lay* is functioning in a different way—as the past tense of *lie*.

Example 1: Jay came home last night and **lay** on the couch. (Past tense)

Example 2: After exercising yesterday, I **lay** on the floor and fell asleep. (Past tense)

Now logically, since *lie* is an intransitive verb, the past tense of *lie*, which is *lay,* as we just used it, must also be intransitive; but only when it is the past tense of lie. (It has no object.) Here we have dealt with yet another word with more than one function. Of course, you know of many other words like *lay and lie*; but with these two, people pay scant attention to their unique differences and choose to use them incorrectly.

Incorrect: Riley, come and ~~lay~~ on your bed.

Correct: Riley, come and **lie** on your bed.

Incorrect: There is a man ~~laying~~ in the street and no one is helping him. (I heard this at news time on TV recently.)

Correct: There is a man **lying** in the street and no one is helping him.

Their after The Antecedent

Pronouns must agree with their antecedents, the nouns for which they stand, in number, person and gender. Therefore, the plural pronoun, *their*, should not refer to a singular noun.

Antecedent   Pronoun

Example*: Children must be taught to put **their** toys away after pla*y. (Correct)

In this sentence, both the antecedent and the pronoun referring to the antecedent are plural, as they should be. However, the construction we find to be most prevalent is one like this:

A **child** must be taught to put ~~their~~ toys away after

play. (Incorrect)

Here, the antecedent, *child*, and the pronoun *their* referring to *child* are not in step with each other. One is singular and the other is plural. This often occurs when the antecedent, as in this case, is the common gender—belonging to either sex.

A Possible Correction: A child must be taught to put **his** or **her** toys away after play. We agree that this construction is unwieldy and for this same reason, I am sure, many people make the decision to use *their* with wild abandon in these constructions, whether the sentence is grammatically correct or not. Once, when it was not politically incorrect to do so, one could write:

*A **child** must be taught to put ~~his~~ toys away after play.*

In this sentence the antecedent is singular and so, too, is the pronoun that follows. This construction allows the use of the masculine gender as a generic form for both male and female. This is frowned upon today—as it should be; but certainly not to the further detriment of the language.

I remember an incident when, fresh from another culture, I attempted to use such a construction within the hallowed walls of a prestigious Washington DC University and immediately incurred the righteous wrath of the female professor there. I never did it again.

But here's a fairly acceptable alternative. If you insist on using the plural pronoun, **their,** then you will need to make the antecedent plural also:

Children *must be taught to put* **their** *toys away after play.*

In regard to or with regard to not in ~~regards~~ to and not with ~~regards~~ to

Whenever there is the inclination to say *in regards to* or *with regards to,* just drop the *s* on ~~regards.~~

Etc. at the end of a list. Etc. *etcetera* is Latin for **and so on, and others of the same kind.** If no other of the same kind comes to mind, end the list before the addition of **etc.**

Review and Practice Time

1. **Choose from these words to fill the blanks:** lie, lay, amount, an, a, number, is, **are**:

    1) She said she would be here in ___ hour's time.
    2) He is ___ honest man.
    3) Each team that ran _____ race won ___ medal.
    4) This is _____ opportunity to improve your grade in the class.
    5) We found a _____ of empty bottles in a box.
    6) They deposited a large _____ of sand on the sidewalk.
    7) Every day, I _____ my hat beside me as I _____ in the shade at the beach.
    8) There _____ beautiful paintings in this room.
    9) There _____ a number of small streams throughout the farmland.
    10) Last evening, I arrived home, _____ on the couch, and fell fast asleep.

2. Rewrite or fill the blanks with the right words.

1.) My shoes are different _____ hers.

_____

2.) The sermon was centered _____ the meaning of
Christmas.

_____

3.) One letter grade is lost if a student submits _____
assignments late.

_____

7

Those who write clearly have readers; those who write obscurely have commentators.
—Albert Camus, French Novelist, Essayist, 1957 Nobel Prize for Literature. (1913-1960)

Pull the Plug on Poor Punctuation

- The Apostrophe
- The Apostrophe in Contractions
- The Apostrophe used to Show Possession
- Pronouns never need the Apostrophe
- The Ellipsis Dots

In order to write clearly it is necessary to have, in addition to an understanding of the rules of grammar, a firm grasp of the rules that govern punctuation. Before we venture further, here is a reminder: Punctuation and grammar are two distinct areas of study. I have heard and seen people treat these two as though they are the same. Without the ability to use punctuation well, much of what we write could be easily misunderstood.

The following is a well-known example of the perils of poor punctuation.

Woman without her man is nothing.
Woman! Without her, man is nothing.

Observe how the placement of punctuation marks in these two sentences makes an interesting difference to their meanings. Here is another example of this:

Let us eat John.
Let us eat, John.

Which is it? Are you about to eat John or are you and John about to have a meal together? Be very careful how you punctuate, less you find yourself communicating something you did not intend.

The Apostrophe (')

The punctuation mark which seems to be most often misused is the apostrophe. Rather than deal with all the many abuses of the apostrophe here, let us instead grapple with the ones that I have regularly encountered.

WordSmith.com, a worldwide online community of over half a million readers who share a love for words, wordplay, language, and literature had this to say about the apostrophe:

> We don't put them where they belong, and we add them where they don't. Sometimes we are not sure whether an apostrophe is needed, so we simply add one, as if considering pillars to support a roof.

Unfortunately, this is true of the way some people use the apostrophe. According to *WordSmith*, in the same article, "too many people seem intent on liberally sprinkling the little curly monsters over everything they write"—or, I think, they leave them out entirely as if they had neither heard of their existence, nor of their usefulness in well written material. Here we will concern ourselves with two important functions of the apostrophe: How we use it in some contractions and how we use it to show possession.

The Apostrophe in Contractions

If I were to borrow the words of the popular song from the movie, *The Sound of Music* I would consider the contraction as "a very good place to start." So, "let's start at the very beginning".

The term *contraction* hints at a shrinking and this is exactly what we do when, instead of writing *it is*, we write *it's*. Again, instead of writing *would not*, you write *won't* or *wouldn't*. In the contraction, two words become one word with the help of the apostrophe and the omission of some letters.

Could've

A contraction that people sometimes use incorrectly is **could've.** This error is not noticeable until the "perpetrator" is asked to write what was just said. Then instead of the *could've,* we see ~~could of.~~

Incorrect: I ~~could of~~ danced all night.

Correct: I **could've** danced all night. (I **could have** danced all night.)

You're Welcome

This is the response to "Thank you." We say, or should say, "You're welcome."

In some cases, we think that the right thing was said. However, if the response is put on a page, we will surely see, "~~Your~~ welcome."

Incorrect: ~~Your~~ welcome.

Correct: You're welcome. (You are welcome.)

It's and Its

It's is a contraction meaning *it is* or *it has*.

Example 1: It's a beautiful day.

Example 2: It's been a long time since I last saw you.

These are two distinct words, a subject and verb unit. The first word, *it*, is the subject and the second word *is* or *has* is the verb.

The Apostrophe to Show Possession

Example 1. *The child's book is on the desk.* (Singular Possessive)

Here we have one book belonging to one child.

Example 2. *The children's books are on the desks.* (Plural Possessive)

We all know that the word, *child,* does not become plural by adding an *s* at the end like this (~~childs~~); instead it becomes a new word, *child***ren**. Therefore, to form the plural possessive, we only need to add an *apostrophe and s* after the word, *child***ren,** like this: *child***ren's**.

Example 3.
(a) *The girl's dress was beautiful.* (Singular Possessive)
(b) *The girl's dresses were beautiful* (Singular *Possessive*)

Example 4.
The girls' dresses were beautiful. (Plural Possessive)

The plural of girl, *girls,* already has an *s* at the end; therefore add the apostrophe after the *s* to show possession (girls').

Notice that the item or items possessed never determine the placement of the *apostrophe and the s*, but the possessor does—depending on whether that possessor is one or more than one (singular or plural).

There is a lot more to be learned about nouns and the possessive. But for our purpose we will close this section with the treatment of proper nouns:

Richard's car (Singular Possessive)
Charles' car (Singular Possessive)

Again, if the name ends with an *s* add only an apostrophe. Some authorities also require that we write, instead, *Charles's car.*

Did you notice that we have been dealing only with nouns and the possessive so far? This is because only nouns undergo this change to show possession—the change made with the addition of the apostrophe and s. or, with an s followed by an apostrophe.

The Apostrophe that Pronouns Never Need

The <u>dog</u> wags its <u>tail</u>.
The <u>book</u> has lost its <u>cover</u>.

The word, *its,* in these two sentences, is one word, not a contraction of two words; and therefore needs no apostrophe.

The tail belongs to the dog and the possessive pronoun, *its,* shows the relationship between the two nouns, *dog* and *tail.* In the second sentence also, *its* shows the relationship between the cover and the book and is not a contraction. Do not use an apostrophe. Disregard the yearning to do so. The compulsion will go away eventually. If you did add an apostrophe, your sentence would mean:

The dog wags ~~it is~~ tail.
The book has lost ~~it is~~ cover.
Surely, that is not what you meant to say or write.

Here is a list of possessive pronouns:**Mine, yours, ours, his, hers, theirs, its**.

I purposely put *mine* at the beginning of the list, so that some of the people I have "fought" with to abandon the addition of an apostrophe and *s* to this word—if they read these pages—will remember and perhaps smile at the memory. The truth is this: There is no word like ~~mine's~~.

Pronouns, as a general rule, never use an apostrophe to show possession the way nouns do. We say and write *the dog's tail.* Dog is a noun and uses the *apostrophe and s* to show possession; but we say and write **its tail** with no apostrophe and *s* on the pronoun, *its*, to show possession.

Well, some may say, here's the pronoun, *she* with an apostrophe and *s* added to it:

Gayle is here. **She's** *at the door.*

Yes; but *she's* means *she is,* another example of a subject (she) and verb (is) combination. There is no hint of possession here.

A Short Diversion

A charming, but mischievous, young lady in one of my classes some time ago, eventually got it right, but would revert to "~~mine's~~", with an emphasis on the word, whenever she felt like annoying me during the two-week-long training class. I never let her know how successful she was each time she did that.

The Ellipsis Dots

Ellipsis dots (plural ellipses) indicate the omission of words or an entire paragraph from a quotation. We use three dots . . . to show these omissions, but four dots if the omission comes after a complete sentence, in which case the first dot is actually the period used after the completed sentence. They are each separated by a space.

There is wide-spread misuse of the ellipsis and apparently for no reason other than to decorate a page. In this regard, it seems the ellipsis has now joined the apostrophe in the race for most used, ill used, and abused, punctuation.

Three Ellipsis Dots

Example 1:

I had forty cousins yet I was the only one who went to college. They were affluent, but they put   absolutely no premium on education. They valued street wiles, street smarts, never education. So I faced a blank screen . . . no preconceptions, restrictions, or restraints.

—Roger Gould, Author and Psychoanalyst
(taken from Warren Bennis' book *On Becoming A Leader*)

Notice that the <u>three dots</u> begin after a space following the last letter in the word *screen* and end before the space with the first letter in the word *no*. This indicates that words were left out after "screen" and before "no". Those words were not needed in the quote.

Example 2: Most people know that the *Declaration of Independence* begins with the following sentence:

"When, in the course of human events . . ."

When quoting from this document in a written exercise, you may find it difficult to remember other lines of the document. The use of the ellipsis here shows there is more to follow. In this particular case, as we well know, there is much more to follow.

Four Ellipsis Dots (Really three ellipsis dots and one period)

Example 1:

*We have also come to this hallowed spot to remind America of the fierce urgency of **Now**. . . . **Now** is the time to make real the promises of democracy."*

—Dr. Martin Luther King, Jr. (1929-1968)

Here, the four dots include the period after the sentence ending with the first ***now***. Notice also that after the first ***now*** there is no space before the period, because it is a period and not an ellipsis dot.

There is much more about the ellipsis dots, but this satisfies our purpose here. Take the time to remember what was said here about the ellipsis, and you will be able, not only to use this punctuation correctly, but you will use it only when it is necessary.

Review and Practice Time

1. **Fill the blanks below with *its* or *it's*.**
   1.) Carol returned the report to _____ folder.
   2.) The <u>lark</u> sang _____ beautiful <u>song</u>.
   3.) My dress is missing all _____ buttons.

2. **Change the following sentences to the Plural Possessive**
   1.) The man's pen is on the desk.
   2.) John painted the angel's wings before going to bed.
   3.) The book's cover was beautifully designed.
   4.) The newspaper's review of our Christmas concert was good.

3. **Fill the blanks by choosing the correct word for each sentence:**
   Vanessa's, yours, mine, his, could've, its, it's, you're, your, Ryan's.
   1) _____ a long way from here to the bank.
   2) "Thank you," he said. I replied, "_____ welcome."
   3) I _____ arrived here earlier; but my train was late.
   4) The bird feeds _____ young until they are able to fly from the nest.
   5) This book is _____ and that one is _____.
   6) Please write _____ name on this form.
   7) I placed _____ shirt on _____ hanger and hung it in _____ closet.
   8) _____ choreography and costumes for the show were well applauded.

3. **When would you use the three-dot ellipsis?**

8

In this world one must be like everybody else if [one] doesn't want to provoke scorn or envy or jealousy.
—Mark Twain, American author and humorist (1835-1910)

Epilogue

We've come to the end of this work; but I cannot consider it complete until I include this last and important bit of information. It deals with a.m. and p.m. and I have named it:

That Time of Day

No. I have not veered from the subject by injecting this here. I really consider this vital to good communication. Too many people seem content with a level of inaccuracy when giving the time of day that is associated with the midday hour (noon) and/or midnight. Let us, therefore, examine the corrected forms and be mindful of the importance of getting them right at all times, especially in communicating critical or time-sensitive information.

Be warned: There is no 12:00 a.m., nor is there a 12:00 p.m; yet people use them every day. These are vague terms with the potential of causing confusion in the minds of others and should not be used. We should say, instead, 12:00 noon and 12:00 midnight.

The abbreviation for *Anti Meridiem* (Latin) meaning before midday is A.M. and P.M is the abbreviation for *Post Meridiem* (Latin) meaning after midday. One minute after 12:00 noon will be 12:01 **p.m.** and likewise one minute after 12:00 midnight will be 12:01 **a.m.** It has been reported that some airlines and insurance companies wisely use 12:01a.m to identify the start of the day and 11:59 p.m. as the end of the day.

New Horizons

Now, may I ask that you put some of these ideas into practice? Do the Review and Practice Time exercises found at the end of all chapters—except the first and last, check your answers at the back of the book and move confidently in the new direction that you've chosen.

There is nothing wrong with being different. We are all different from each other in many ways, but also uncannily alike in others. The real aim here, however, is not to provoke scorn or envy—remember Mark Twain was also a humorist—but to be more effective, a state of being which could be extremely rewarding and thoroughly enjoyable, too. I hope that, as you work diligently through the pages of this book, you will gain more assurance in your skills to communicate effectively.

Do not to be deterred by the frequent mention of the grammatical rules of the language. I have injected the grammar only to explain some of the difficulties you may encounter along the way and, also, to eventually wean you from a dependency on rote. Independently, you will be able to decide whether a construction is right or wrong, because of your own awareness of the rules that govern that construction.

I have heard it said that some people use their knowledge of grammar as a means of elevating themselves to a certain level of snobbery. That is not our goal. Instead, we are using the rules of grammar as a means of attaining a natural correctness of expression that puts us "ahead of the pack".

This naturalness will only increase your confidence and credibility as you go about your daily lives— communicating with colleagues, business partners or customers in the work environment, shining at an important interview; writing that important report, or even as you mingle with friends and acquaintances in a social setting.

Yet, in spite of your efforts at good communication, always be cognizant of the fact that communication does not always take place. At times, for many reasons, a miscommunication occurs. We say something to a friend, colleague or other and unknown to both of you the message sent is not the one received. The moment passes and you move on to other things with a miscommunication left hanging out there, unresolved.

The ability to use the language efficiently is powerful and rewarding. But even as we endeavor to perfect our speaking and writing roles, we need to remember that there is yet another important element waiting to be embraced. It is Active Listening.

Active Listening is the kind of listening in which you are completely involved with both the messenger and the message. It is an art that must be practiced and an integral part of good communication skills.

Truly, in writing this book I am merely opening the door for you to experience much more as you enter. Therefore, do not be satisfied with the little you have gleaned here. Instead, open wide the door, enter, and feast on the wonders within the welcoming halls of knowledge.

If your interest in this subject has peaked as a result of reading these pages, then, you will continue in earnestness from the point at which this book concludes. By so doing, you will have helped me accomplish my objective in writing this, even as you hone and enhance your own skills in communication. I thank you for staying the course.

Answers to Review and Practice Time

2 Let's Wage a War on "Words"

Page 18

1. Affidavit
2. Conversing
3. Regardless
4. Crises
5. Alzheimer's

3 Render Results with Rules

Page 23

1.) Jack and Jill
2.) Rylie and Ayden
3.) Kailey
4.) The white cat
5.) (You)
6.) My family

Subject	Predicate
1) Little Bo-Peep	<u>has lost</u> her sheep.
2) I	<u>ate</u> the cherries yesterday.
3) (You)	jump!
4) Jack and Jill	<u>went</u> up the hill.
5) Rylie and Ayden	practice their steps every day.
6) Kailey	*understands* graphs well.
7) The white cat	*is sleeping on my bed.*
8) My family	<u>loves</u> me.

4. Rules Still Rule the Roost

Page 34
1.
1) me
2) me
3) I
4) I
5) me
6) I
7) I

2.
a) **Direct Object:** doughnuts
b) **Indirect Object:** her sister and me

c) **Direct Object:** a beautiful ring
d) **Indirect Object:** his mother

3.

Subject	Predicate		
	Verb	Object	Extension
The children	were playing	_____	in the park (place) yesterday (time)
I	put	fresh flowers	in my vases (place) every week (time)
The little girl and her mother	ran		up the stairs (place) quickly (manner)
We	went		to a restaurant (place) after the concert (time)

5. Words Need a Relationship

Page 52
1.
1) Knows
2) Knew
3) Had known

2.

Correct: She <u>does</u> the dishes.

3.

1) Have done
2) Has gone
3) Had come
4) Have sung

4.

1) Writes. . . . . .write
1) walks. . . . . .walk

5.

1) There is
2) There are
3) There are
4) There are
5) There is

6.

1) I
2) I
3) I
4) I

7. Nouns: 1) Lady, dress, patio
2) Man, walk
3) Children, clowns, stage, circus
4) Breakfast
6) Game, players, ball, fence
7) Kick, ball, stands
8) Meg, exercise, homework

Pronouns: 1) We,
2) They
3) She, you
8) She

Verbs: 1) Saw, walk
2) Rested
3) Applauded, entered
4) Exercise
5) Exclaimed, are
6) Kick
7) Sent
8) Has completed, had

Adjectives: 1) Young, red,
2) Old, long
6) High
7) First

Adverbs: 1) Slowly
3) Loudly
5) There
6) Quickly

Prepositions: 1) In, across
2) After
3) At
4) Before
6) Before, over
7) Into

Conjunctions: 3) As

Interjections: 5) Ah!

6. A Choice of Words

Page 64
1.
  1) An
  2) An
  3) A, a
  4) An
  5) Number
  6) Amount
  7) Lay, lie
  8) Are
  9) Is
  10) Lay

2.
  1) Different <u>from</u>
  2) Centered <u>on</u>
  3) One letter grade is lost if students submit their assignments late.

7. Pull the Plug on Poor Punctuation

Page 74
1.
  1) Carol returned the report to its <u>folder</u>.
  2) Paul gave the <u>kitten</u> to its <u>owner</u>.
  3) The <u>lark</u> sang its beautiful <u>song</u>.

2.
  1) The men's pens are on the desk.
  2) John painted the angels' wings before going to bed.
  3) The books' covers were beautifully designed.

4) The newspapers' reviews of our Christmas concert were good.

1) It's a long way from here to the bank.
2) "Thank you," he said.
I replied, "You're welcome."
3) I could've arrived here earlier; but my train was late.
4) The bird feeds its young until they are able to fly from the nest.
5) This book is yours and that one is mine.
6) Please write your name on this form.
7) I placed Ryan's shirt on its hanger and hung it in his closet.
8) Vanessa's choreography and costumes for the show were well applauded.

Bibliography

American-Speech-Language-Hearing Association http://www.asha.org/slp/ Retrieved 7/12/2008.

A Word A Day with Anu Garg. http://wordsmith.org. Retrieved 1.09.2009 and 6/18/2008.

Bennis, Warren G. *On Becoming A Leader.* Reading, Mass. Addison-Wesley Publishing, 1994.

Ehrlich, Eugene and Hawes, Gene. *Speak for Success.* Toronto, New York, London: Bantam Books. 1984.

http://eslus.com/LESSONS/GRAMMAR/POS/pos1.htm. *Interlink Language Center.* Retrieved 6/15/2008.

http://grammar.ccc.commnet.edu/grammar/to_be.htm. Forms of the verb "to be". Retrieved 6/20/09.

http://linguistlist.org/issues/13/13-3353.html. Steve Moran, "ed." Retrieved 9/20/2008.

http://www.workinghumor.com/quotes/winston_churchill.
shtml. *Humorous Quotes Attributed to Winston
Churchill.* Retrieved 8/15/2009.

http://www.worldtimezone.com/wtz-names/wtz-am-pm.
html. Retrieved 5/12/2008.

Oxford English Reference Dictionary. Second Edition
Revised. Great Clarendon St. Oxford.Oxford
University Press. (2003).

The Chicago Manual of Style, Fifteenth Edition. Chicago
and London. The University of Chicago. (2003).

Waldhorn, Arthur, PhD, and Zeiger, Arthur, PhD. "advisory
editors", *English Made Simple.* London. UK.
Heinemann (1981).

Webster's Ninth New Collegiate Dictionary. Springfield,
Mass. Merriam-Webster Inc. 1990.